Data Source Handbook

Data Source Handbook

Pete Warden

Beijing · Cambridge · Farnham · Köln · Sebastopol · Tokyo

Data Source Handbook

by Pete Warden

Published by O'Reilly Media, Inc., 1005 Gravenstein Highway North, Sebastopol, CA 95472.

O'Reilly books may be purchased for educational, business, or sales promotional use. Online editions are also available for most titles (*http://my.safaribooksonline.com*). For more information, contact our corporate/institutional sales department: (800) 998-9938 or *corporate@oreilly.com*.

Editor: Mike Loukides

Production Editor: Teresa Elsey

Proofreader: Teresa Elsey

Cover Designer: Karen Montgomery

Interior Designer: David Futato

Illustrator: Robert Romano

Printing History:

February 2011:   First Edition.

ISBN: 978-1-449-30314-3

[LSI]

1295991502

Table of Contents

Preface

A lot of new sources of free, public data have emerged over the last few years, and this guide covers some of the most useful. It's aimed at developers looking for information to supplement their own tools or services. There are obviously a lot of APIs out there (*http://programmableweb.com/*), so to narrow it down to the most useful, the ones in this guide have to meet these standards:

Free or self-service signup
> Traditional commercial data agreements are designed for enterprise companies, so they're very costly and time-consuming to experiment with. APIs that are either free or have a simple sign-up process make it a lot easier to get started.

Broad coverage
> Quite a few startups build infrastructure and then hope that users will populate it with data. Most of the time, this doesn't happen, so you end up with APIs that look promising on the surface but actually contain very little useful data.

Online API or downloadable bulk data
> Most of us now develop in the web world, so anything else requires a complex installation process that makes it much harder to try out.

Linked to outside entities
> There has to be some way to look up information that ties the service's data to the outside world. For example, the Twitter and Facebook APIs don't qualify because you can only find users by internal identifiers, whereas LinkedIn does because you can look up accounts by their real-world names and locations.

I also avoid services that impose excessive conditions on what you can do with the information they provide. There are some on the border of acceptability there, so for them I've highlighted any special restrictions on how you can use the data, along with links to the full terms of service.

The APIs are organized by the subject that they cover (for example, websites, people, or places), so you can discover the best sources to augment your data. Please get in touch (*pete@petewarden.com*) if you know of services that are missing, or have other questions or suggestions.

Data Source Handbook

Websites

WHOIS (*http://whois.domaintools.com*)

The whois Unix command is still a workhorse, and I've found the web service a decent alternative, too. You can get the basic registration information for any website. In recent years, some owners have chosen "private" registration, which hides their details from view, but in many cases you'll see a name, address, email, and phone number for the person who registered the site. You can also enter numerical IP addresses here and get data on the organization or individual that owns that server.

Unfortunately the terms of service of most providers forbid automated gathering and processing of this information, but you can craft links to the Domain Tools site to make it easy for your users to access the information:

```
<a href="http://whois.domaintools.com/www.google.com">Info for www.google.com</a>
```

There is a commercial API available through whoisxmlapi.com (*http://www.whoisxmlapi.com/*) that offers a JSON interface and bulk downloads, which seems to contradict the terms mentioned in most WHOIS results. It costs $15 per thousand queries. Be careful, though; it requires you to send your password as a nonsecure URL parameter, so don't use a valuable one:

```
curl "http://www.whoisxmlapi.com/whoisserver/WhoisService?\
domainName=oreilly.com&outputFormat=json&userName=<username>&password=<password>"
{"WhoisRecord": {
  "createdDate": "26-May-97",
  "updatedDate": "26-May-10",
  "expiresDate": "25-May-11",
  "registrant": {
    "city": "Sebastopol",
    "state": "California",
    "postalCode": "95472",
    "country": "United States",
    "rawText": "O'Reilly Media, Inc.\u000a1005 Gravenstein Highway North
\u000aSebastopol, California 95472\u000aUnited States\u000a",
```

```
    "unparsable": "O'Reilly Media, Inc.\u000a1005 Gravenstein Highway North"
  },
  "administrativeContact": {
    "city": "Sebastopol",
...
```

Blekko (*http://blekko.com*)

The newest search engine in town, Blekko sells itself on the richness of the data it offers. If you type in a domain name followed by /seo, you'll receive a page of statistics on that URL (Figure 1).

Inbound links: 6,121 from 532 domains:

#	from host	host rank	links	last	actions
1	www.google.com	12,932	6		
2	twitter.com	12,366.4	6		
3	www.flickr.com	9,179.3	1		
4	www.guardian.co.uk	6,481.2	1		
5	groups.google.com	4,102.7	2		
6	www.msnbc.msn.com	3,771.4	1	329d ago	
7	www.forbes.com	3,699.8	1	65d ago	

Figure 1. Blekko statistics

Blekko is also very keen on developers accessing its data, so it offers an easy-to-use API through the /json slash tag, which returns a JSON object instead of HTML:

```
http://blekko.com/?q=cure+for+headaches+/json+/ps=100&auth=<APIKEY>&ft=&p=1
```

To obtain an API key, email *apiauth@blekko.com*. The terms of service are available at *https://blekko.com/ws/+/terms*, and while they're somewhat restrictive, they are flexible in practice:

> You should note that it prohibits practically all interesting uses of the blekko API. We are not currently issuing formal written authorization to do things prohibited in the agreement, but, if you are well behaved (e.g., not flooding us with queries), and we know your email address (from when you applied for an API auth key, see above), we will have the ability to attempt to contact you and discuss your usage patterns if needed.

Currently, the /seo results aren't available through the JSON interface, so you have to scrape the HTML to obtain them. There's a demonstration of that at *https://github.com/petewarden/pagerankgraph*.

bit.ly (*http://code.google.com/p/bitly-api/wiki/ApiDocumentation*)

The bit.ly API (*http://code.google.com/p/bitly-api/wiki/ApiDocumentation*) lets you access analytics information for a URL that's been shortened. If you're starting off with a full URL, you'll need to call the lookup function (*http://code.google.com/p/bitly-api/wiki/ApiDocumentation#/v3/lookup*) to obtain the short URL. You can sign up for API access here (*http://bit.ly/a/sign_up*). This is most useful if you want to gauge the popularity of a site, either so you can sort and filter links you're displaying to a user or to feed into your own analysis algorithms:

```
curl "http://api.bit.ly/v3/clicks?login=<login>&apiKey=<key>&\
shortUrl=http://bit.ly/hnB7HI"
```

```
{"status_code": 200, "data": {
  "clicks": [{
    "short_url": "http://bit.ly/hnB7HI",
    "global_hash": "gKGd7s",
    "user_clicks": 9,
    "user_hash": "hnB7HI",
    "global_clicks": 36}]},
  "status_txt": "OK"
}
```

Compete (*http://developer.compete.com/*)

The Compete API (*http://developer.compete.com/*) gives a very limited amount of information on domains, a trust rating, a ranking for how much traffic a site receives, and any online coupons associated with the site. Unfortunately, you don't get the full traffic history information that powers the popular graphs on the web interface. The terms of service (*http://developer.compete.com/Api_terms_of_use*) also rate-limit you to 1,000 calls a day, and you can't retain any record of the information you pull, which limits its usefulness:

```
curl "http://api.compete.com/fast-cgi/MI?d=google.com&ver=3&apikey=<key>&size=large"

<ci>
      <dmn>
            <nm>google.com</nm>
            <trust caption="Trust">
                  <val>green</val>
                  <link>http://toolbar.compete.com/trustgreen/google.com</link>
            <icon>...</icon>
            </trust>
            <rank caption="Profile">
                  <val>1</val>
                  <link>http://toolbar.compete.com/siteprofile/google.com</link>
                <icon>...</icon>
            </rank>
      ...
```

Delicious (*http://www.delicious.com/help/json*)

Despite its uncertain future, the Delicious service collects some of the most useful information on URLs I've found. The API returns the top 10 tags for any URL, together with a count of how many times each tag has been used (Figure 2).

Figure 2. Delicious tags

You don't need a key to use the API, and it supports JSONP callbacks, allowing you to access it even within completely browser-based applications. Here's some PHP sample code on github (*http://github.com/petewarden/delicious_tags*), but the short version is you call to *http://feeds.delicious.com/v2/json/urlinfo/data?hash=* with the MD5 hash of the URL appended, and you get back a JSON string containing the tags:

```
md5 -s http://petewarden.typepad.com/
MD5 ("http://petewarden.typepad.com/") = 7527287d9d937c59a3250ef3a60671f3

curl "http://feeds.delicious.com/v2/json/urlinfo/data?\
hash=7527287d9d937c59a3250ef3a60671f3"

[{
   "hash":"7527287d9d937c59a3250ef3a60671f3",
   "title":"PeteSearch",
   "url":"http:\/\/petewarden.typepad.com\/",
   "total_posts":78,
   "top_tags":{"analytics":29,"blog":28,"data":26,"facebook":20,
"programming":18,"social":13,"blogs":13,"search":12,"visualization":8,"analysis":8}
}]
```

BackType (*http://www.backtype.com/developers*)

BackType (*http://www.backtype.com/*) keeps track of the public conversations associated with a web page and offers an API (*http://www.backtype.com/developers/connect*) to retrieve them from your own service. The service rate-limits to 1,000 calls a day, but from talking to BackType, it seems they're keen to help if you want higher usage (*http://www.backtype.com/contact*).

The information is usually used to display related conversations in a web interface, but, with a bit of imagination, you could use it to identify users related to a particular topic or gauge the popularity of a page instead:

```
curl "http://api.backtype.com/connect.json?\
url=http://www.techcrunch.com/2009/03/30/if-bitly-is-worth-8-million-tinyurl-is\
-worth-at-least-46-million/&key=0cd9bd64b6dc4e4186b9"
```

```
{"startindex":1,"itemsperpage":25,"next_page":2,"comments":[{"comment":
{"id":"000032ca7e8b26f9d79b549cb451b518",
  "url":"http:\/\/blog.saush.com\/2009\/04\/13\/
clone-tinyurl-in-40-lines-of-ruby-code\/#comment-1476",
  "content":"...",
  "date":"2010-12-06 17:10:53"},
  "blog":{"id":13002,
   "url":"http:\/\/blog.saush.com\/","title":"saush.com"},
  "post":{"url":"http:\/\/blog.saush.com\/2009\/04\/13\/
clone-tinyurl-in-40-lines-of-ruby-code\/",
    "title":"Clone TinyURL in 40 lines of Ruby code"},
  "author":{"name":"Cpchhukout",
 "url":"http:\/\/newwave.hoha.ru\/maxim_axenov?ref=wmbasta"},
...
```

PagePeeker (*http://pagepeeker.com/favicons_api.php*)

If you're displaying a lot of URLs to your users, it can be handy to give them visual cues. This simple web service gives you an easy way to do that by embedding HTML images of site favicons:

```
<img src="http://pagepeeker.com/f/wikipedia.org" border="0" width="16px"
height="16px">
```

People by Email

These services let you find information about users on their systems using an email address as a search term. Since it's common to have email addresses for your own users, it's often possible to fetch additional data on them from their other public profiles. For example, if you retrieve a location, real name, portrait, or description from an external service, you can use it to prepopulate your own "create a profile" page. You can find open source code examples demonstrating how to use most of these APIs at *http://*

github.com/petewarden/findbyemail, and there's a live web demo at *http://web.mailana .com/labs/findbyemail/*.

WebFinger (*http://code.google.com/p/webfinger/*)

WebFinger is a unified API that you can use to discover additional information about a person based on his or her email address. It's very much focused on the discovery protocol, and it doesn't specify much about the format of the data returned. It's supported by Google (*https://groups.google.com/group/webfinger/browse_thread/thread/ fb56537a0ed36964*), Yahoo (*http://groups.google.com/group/webfinger/browse_thread/ thread/3f057e12490e45d3*) and AOL (*http://practicalid.blogspot.com/2010/08/webfin ger-enabled-for-aolcom.html*). You can also see PHP source code demonstrating how client code can call the protocol (*https://github.com/petewarden/findbyemail/blob/mas ter/webfinger.php*). It's a REST interface, it returns its results in XML format, and it doesn't require any authentication or keys to access.

Flickr (*http://www.flickr.com/services/api/flickr.people.findByEmail.html*)

As a widely used service, the Flickr REST/XML API is a great source of information on email addresses. You'll see a location, real name, and portrait for people with public profiles, and you'll be able to suggest linking their Flickr accounts with your own site. You'll need to register as a developer (*http://www.flickr.com/services/apps/create/ap ply*) before you can access the interface:

```
curl "http://api.flickr.com/services/rest/?\
method=flickr.people.findByEmail&api_key=<key>&find_email=tim%40oreilly.com"

<?xml version="1.0" encoding="utf-8" ?>
<rsp stat="ok">
<user id="36521959321@N01" nsid="36521959321@N01">
        <username>timoreilly</username>
</user>
</rsp>

curl "http://api.flickr.com/services/rest/?\
method=flickr.people.getInfo&api_key=<key>&user_id=36521959321@N01"

<?xml version="1.0" encoding="utf-8" ?>
<rsp stat="ok">
<person id="36521959321@N01" nsid="36521959321@N01"
 ispro="1" iconserver="1362" iconfarm="2" path_alias="timoreilly">
        <username>timoreilly</username>
        <realname>Tim O'Reilly</realname>
        <location>Sebastopol, CA, USA</location>
        <photosurl>http://www.flickr.com/photos/timoreilly/</photosurl>
        <profileurl>http://www.flickr.com/people/timoreilly/</profileurl>
        <mobileurl>http://m.flickr.com/photostream.gne?id=10317</mobileurl>
        <photos>
                <firstdatetaken>2002-08-03 13:40:04</firstdatetaken>
                <firstdate>1093117877</firstdate>
```

```
            <count>1379</count>
        </photos>
    </person>
    </rsp>
```

Gravatar (*http://en.gravatar.com/site/implement/images/*)

This service lets you pass in an MD5 hash of an email address, and for registered users, it will return a portrait image. Thanks to its integration with Wordpress, quite a few people have signed up, so it can be a good way of providing at least default avatars for your own users. You could also save yourself some coding by directing new users to Gravatar's portrait creation interface. There's also a profile lookup API (*http://en.grav atar.com/site/implement/profiles/*) available, but I haven't had any experience with how well-populated this is:

```
md5 -s pete@mailana.com
MD5 ("pete@mailana.com") = 03e801b74b01f23957a3afdd9aaaed00

<img src="http://www.gravatar.com/avatar/03e801b74b01f23957a3afdd9aaaed00" />
```

Figure 3. Gravatar portrait image

Amazon (*http://docs.amazonwebservices.com/AWSECommerceService/ 2007-08-27/DG/CustomerContentSearch.html*)

Like Yahoo!, Amazon doesn't expose very much information about each user when you look up an email address, but you can often get at least a location. The sheer size of Amazon's user base means that you'll find information on a large percentage of emails. There's also the chance to discover public wishlists, which could be helpful for creating default interests for your new users' profiles.

The API is REST/XML-based, but it does require a somewhat complex URL signing scheme (*http://www.a2sdeveloper.com/page-rest-authentication-for-php4.html*) for authentication.

AIM (*http://x.aim.com/OpenAIMPresentation/*)

You can look up an AOL Instant Messenger account from an email address, and you get a portrait image and username back. The exact information returned depends on whether the user is online, and you'll only get a default image if he or she is away. The service uses a REST/JSON API, and it requires a sign up (*http://developer.aim.com/ manageKeys.jsp*) to access:

```
curl "http://api.oscar.aol.com/presence/get?f=json&k=<key>&\
t=petewarden%40aol.com&emailLookup=1&notFound=1"
```

```
{"response":{"statusCode":200, "statusText":"Ok", "data":{"users":[{
   "emailId":"petewarden@aol.com",
   "aimId":"petewarden",
   "displayId":"petewarden",
   "state":"offline",
   "userType":"aim",
   "presenceIcon":"http://o.aolcdn.com/aim/img/offline.gif"
}]}}}
```

FriendFeed (*http://friendfeed.com/api/documentation*)

FriendFeed never had a lot of users, but many influential early adopters signed up and created profiles including their other accounts. This makes it a great source of Twitter and Facebook account information on tech-savvy users, since you can look up their FriendFeed accounts by email address, and then pull down the other networks they mention in their profiles. It's a REST/JSON interface, and it doesn't require any authentication or developer signup to access:

```
curl "http://friendfeed.com/api/feed/user?emails=tim%40oreilly.com"
```

```
{
...
"user":{"profileUrl":"http://friendfeed.com/timoreilly",
   "matchedEmail":"tim@oreilly.com",
   "nickname":"timoreilly",
   "id":"d85e8470-25c5-11dd-9ea1-003048343a40",
   "name":"Tim O'Reilly"}
}]}
```

```
curl "http://friendfeed.com/api/user/timoreilly/profile"
```

```
{"status":"public","name":"Tim O'Reilly",
...
"services":[
{"url":"http://en.wikipedia.org/wiki/Blog","iconUrl":"...",
 "id":"blog","profileUrl":"http://radar.oreilly.com","name":"Blog"},
{"username":"timoreilly","name":"Disqus","url":"http://www.disqus.com/",
 "profileUrl":"http://www.disqus.com/people/timoreilly/","iconUrl":"...","id":"disqus"},
{"username":"timoreilly","name":"Flickr","url":"http://www.flickr.com/",
 "profileUrl":"http://www.flickr.com/photos/36521959321%40N01/",
 "iconUrl":"...","id":"flickr"},
{"username":"timoreilly","name":"SlideShare","url":"http://www.slideshare.net/",
 "profileUrl":"http://www.slideshare.net/timoreilly",
 "iconUrl":"...","id":"slideshare"},
{"username":"timoreilly","name":"Twitter","url":"http://twitter.com/",
 "profileUrl":"http://twitter.com/timoreilly",
 "iconUrl":"...","id":"twitter"},
```

```
{"username":"tadghin","name":"YouTube","url":"http://www.youtube.com/",
 "profileUrl":"http://www.youtube.com/profile?user=tadghin",
 "iconUrl":"...","id":"youtube"},
{"url":"http://www.facebook.com/","iconUrl":"...","id":"facebook",
 "profileUrl":"http://www.facebook.com/profile.php?id=544591116",
 "name":"Facebook"}],
"nickname":"timoreilly","id":"d85e8470-25c5-11dd-9ea1-003048343a40"}
```

Google Social Graph (*http://code.google.com/apis/socialgraph/*)

Though it's an early experiment that's largely been superseded by Webfinger, this Google API can still be useful for the rich connection information it exposes for signed-up users. Unfortunately, it's not as well-populated as you might expect. It doesn't require any developer keys to access:

```
curl "http://socialgraph.apis.google.com/lookup?\
q=mailto%3asearchbrowser%40gmail.com&fme=1&edi=1&edo=1&pretty=1&sgn=1&callback="

{ "canonical_mapping": {
  "mailto:searchbrowser@gmail.com": "sgn://mailto/?pk\u003dsearchbrowser@gmail.com"
 },
 "nodes": {
 "sgn://mailto/?pk\u003dsearchbrowser@gmail.com": {
  "attributes": {
  },
  "claimed_nodes": [
  ],
  "unverified_claiming_nodes": [
   "sgn://typepad.com/?ident\u003dpetewarden"
  ],
  "nodes_referenced": {
  },
  "nodes_referenced_by": {
   "sgn://typepad.com/?ident\u003dpetewarden": {
    "types": [
     "me"
    ]
   }
  }
 }
 }
}
```

MySpace (*http://wiki.developer.myspace.com/index.php?title=Open _Search*)

The early social network still holds information on a lot of people, and it exposes a surprisingly large amount, including things like age and gender. This could come in handy if you need to do a demographic analysis of your user base, though with the lack of activity on the site, the information will become less useful as time goes by. You can use the API without any authentication:

```
curl "http://api.myspace.com/opensearch/people?searchBy=email&\
searchTerms=bill%40example.com"
```

```
{"startIndex":"1","itemsPerPage":"10","totalResults":"2",
 "resultCount":"2","searchId":"34848869-de3b-415a-81ab-5df0b1ed82eb","entry":[{
   "id":"myspace.com.person.3430419",
   "displayName":"bill",
   "profileUrl":"http:\/\/www.myspace.com\/3430419",
   "thumbnailUrl":"http:\/\/x.myspacecdn.com\/images\/no_pic.gif",
   "msUserType":"RegularUser",
   "gender":"Female",
   "age":"31",
   "location":"",
   "updated":"12\/12\/2010 6:49:11 PM",
   "isOfficial":"0"},{
   "id":"myspace.com.person.146209268",
   "displayName":"Andy",
   "profileUrl":"http:\/\/www.myspace.com\/146209268",
   "thumbnailUrl":"http:\/\/x.myspacecdn.com\/images\/no_pic.gif",
   "msUserType":"RegularUser",
   "gender":"Male",
   "age":"34",
   "location":"",
   "updated":"3\/26\/2010 1:14:00 PM",
   "isOfficial":"0"}]}
```

Github (*http://develop.github.com/p/users.html*)

If you're targeting people who are likely to be developers, there's a good chance they'll
have github accounts, and if they've opted-in to being found by email address, you'll
be able to pull up their public details. The API doesn't require authorization, or even
registration, and it gives you information on users' companies, real names, locations,
and any linked sites, like blogs:

```
curl "http://github.com/api/v2/xml/user/email/pete%40petewarden.com"
```

```
<?xml version="1.0" encoding="UTF-8"?>
<user>
  <gravatar-id>9cbf603d5f93133178367214f1e091b9</gravatar-id>
  <company>Mailana Inc</company>
  <name>Pete Warden</name>
  <created-at type="datetime">2009-12-03T08:29:50-08:00</created-at>
  <location>Boulder, CO</location>
  <public-repo-count type="integer">26</public-repo-count>
  <public-gist-count type="integer">0</public-gist-count>
  <blog>http://petewarden.typepad.com/</blog>
  <following-count type="integer">0</following-count>
  <id type="integer">161459</id>
  <type>User</type>
  <permission nil="true"></permission>
  <followers-count type="integer">58</followers-count>
  <login>petewarden</login>
  <email>pete@petewarden.com</email>
</user>
```

Rapleaf (*http://www.rapleaf.com/developers/api_docs/personalization/ direct*)

Originally, Rapleaf's API returned information about a person's social networking accounts if you supplied an email, but it has recently switched to offering demographic data on age, gender, income, and address instead. The FindByEmail (*http://github.com/ petewarden/findbyemail*) code still uses the old V2 API. Since the service gathers data without any user involvement (though it does operate an opt out (*https://www.rapleaf .com/people/opt_out*) system), it's been controversial (*http://online.wsj.com/article/ SB10001424052702304410504575560243259416072.html*).

Jigsaw (*http://developer.jigsaw.com/documentation/search_and_get_api _guide/2_Search_API_Resources*)

Another service that collects and aggregates information on people with no involvement from the users, Jigsaw lets you look up people by email address. It returns information on a person's real name, location, phone number, company, and job title, if he or she is in the database.

People by Name

A few services let you look up information from just a name (and possibly a location). These can be handy when you're trying to integrate a traditional offline data set with no electronic identifiers or as a fallback linking online accounts with probable phone and address details.

WhitePages (*http://developer.whitepages.com/docs*)

Based on the most comprehensive online phone book I've found for the US and Canada, the WhitePages API lets you look up people by name, address, or phone number. There's a limit of 200 queries per day, and the results are returned as XML:

```
http://api.whitepages.com/find_person/1.0/?\
firstname=mike;lastname=smith;zip=98101;api_key=API_KEYVAL
```

LinkedIn (*http://developer.linkedin.com/docs/DOC-1191*)

It's not obvious at first glance, but you can use the People Search API to find public profiles for LinkedIn users, even if they're not first- or second-degree connections. You'll need to be logged in through OAuth first, which will allow you to do an *Out of Network* search:

```
http://api.linkedin.com/v1/people-search?first-name=[first name]&\
last-name=[last name]&country-code=[country code]&postal-code=[postal code]&\
facets=network&facet=network,0
```

This will return a set of information from the public profiles of everyone who matches your search. By default this is a very small set of data (only the users' names and IDs), but you can ask for more, including full names, companies, job titles, and general locations, using the field selector syntax:

```
http://api.linkedin.com/v1/people-search:
(people:(id,first-name,last-name,profile-url,headline),num-results
```

GenderFromName (*http://github.com/petewarden/genderfromname*)

A PHP port of a venerable Perl module (*http://search.cpan.org/~edaly/Text-Gender FromName-0.32/GenderFromName.pm*), itself based on an early '90s awk script, this project guesses a person's gender from his or her first name. It's most effective for British and American people, and it has quite an impressive set of battle-tested special-case algorithms to handle a lot of variants and nicknames. Nothing like this will be 100 percent accurate, but it's great for applications like demographic analysis where occasional errors don't matter:

```
require_once('genderfromname.php');

print gender("Jon");    // prints 'm'
```

People by Account

Klout (*http://developer.klout.com/docs/read/api/API*)

Klout's API will give you an influence score for a given Twitter username. You can then use this information to help prioritize Twitter accounts within your own service (for example, by highlighting links shared by people with higher reputation or spam filtering those with low scores):

```
http://api.klout.com/1/klout.xml?key=[your_api_key]&users=[usernames]
```

Qwerly (*http://dev.qwerly.com/docs*)

This service allows you to link Twitter usernames with accounts on other sites. Unfortunately, the data is still pretty sparse, and the Facebook account lookup doesn't return any useful information, but it's still worth a look:

```
curl "http://api.qwerly.com/v1/twitter/petewarden.json?api_key=<key>"
```

```
{ "location":"Boulder, CO",
  "name":"Pete Warden",
  "twitter_username":"petewarden",
  "qwerly_username":null,
  "services":[
    {"type":"github","url":"http://github.com/petewarden","username":"petewarden"},
    {"type":"twitter","url":"http://twitter.com/petewarden","username":"petewarden"},
```

```
    {"type":"klout","url":"http://klout.com/petewarden","username":"petewarden"}
]}
```

Search Terms

Sometimes you're trying to match a word or phrase with some web pages within your service, either for traditional user-driven search or as part of a backend analysis process. The biggest downside of most of the APIs is usually their restrictive terms of service, especially if you're doing further processing with the results instead of showing them directly to users, so make sure you read the fine print. You can find PHP example code for Bing, BOSS, and Google on my blog (*http://petewarden.typepad.com/searchbrowser/ 2009/09/why-i-switched-my-search-api-from-bing-to-google.html*).

BOSS (*http://developer.yahoo.com/search/boss/boss_guide/overview .html*)

One of the earliest search APIs, BOSS is under threat from Yahoo!'s need to cut costs. It's still a great, simple service for retrieving search results, though, with extremely generous usage limits. Its terms of service (*http://info.yahoo.com/legal/us/yahoo/search/ bosstos/bosstos-2317.html*) prohibit anything but user-driven search usage, and you'll need to sign up (*https://developer.apps.yahoo.com/wsregapp/*) to get an API key before you can access it. It offers web, news, and image searches, though the web results are noticeably less complete than Google's, especially on more obscure queries:

```
curl "http://boss.yahooapis.com/ysearch/web/v1/%22Pete%20Warden%22?\
appid=<key>&format=xml"

<?xml version="1.0" encoding="UTF-8"?>
<ysearchresponse xmlns="http://www.inktomi.com/" responsecode="200">
  <nextpage><![CDATA[/ysearch/web/v1/%22Pete%20Warden%22?
format=xml&count=10&appid=<key>&start=10]]></nextpage>
  <resultset_web count="10" start="0" totalhits="6185" deephits="17900">
    <result>
      <abstract><![CDATA[<b>Pete Warden's</b> Video Effects. Free Downloads. Help.
Links. Contact. Free Downloads. PeteSearch <b>...</b> The code is open-source, and
I'm also happy to hand it over to any <b>...</b>]]></abstract>
      <date>2008/04/09</date>
      <dispurl><![CDATA[www.<b>petewarden.com</b>]]></dispurl>
      <size>6173</size>
      <title><![CDATA[<b>Pete Warden</b>]]></title>
      <url>http://www.petewarden.com/</url></result>
...
```

Blekko (*http://blekko.com/*)

As a newcomer to the search space, Blekko seem very keen on developers accessing its data, so it offers an easy-to-use API. All you need to do is add the /json slash tag to any query and you'll get a JSON object instead of HTML:

```
curl -L "http://blekko.com/?q=cure+for+headaches+/json+/ps=100&auth=<APIKEY>&ft=&p=1"

{
   "num_elem_start" : 101,
   "universal_total_results" : "1M",
   "tag_switches" : {
...
   },
   "RESULT" : [
      {
         "snippet" : "Shop By Supplement.  Amino Acid Supplements.  Green Food
Supplements.  Multi-Vitamins &amp; Minerals.  Internal Detox Cleanse.",
         "display_url" : "herbalremedies.com/...-<b><b>for</b>-<b>headaches</b></b>
-don-colbert.html",
         "n_group" : 101,
         "short_host_url" : "http://www.herbalremedies.com/",
         "url_title" : "The Bible <strong><strong>Cure</strong> <strong>for</strong>
<strong>Headaches</strong></strong> by Don Colbert, M.D",
         "c" : 1,
         "short_host" : "herbalremedies.com",
         "url" :
 "http://www.herbalremedies.com/the-bible-cure-for-headaches-don-colbert.html"
      },
   ...
```

To obtain an API key, email *apiauth@blekko.com*. The terms of service (*https://blekko
.com/ws/+/terms*) are somewhat restrictive, but the service is small and hungry enough
to be flexible in practice (at least until it becomes large and well fed).

Bing (*http://www.bing.com/developers*)

Microsoft offers quite a comprehensive set of search APIs for standard web results,
along with images, news, and even local businesses. Though the terms of service (*http:
//www.bing.com/developers/tou.aspx*) make it clear the service is intended only for end-
user-facing websites, the lack of rate limits is very welcome. You'll need to obtain an
API key (*http://www.bing.com/developers/createapp.aspx*) before you can use the API:

```
curl "http://api.bing.net/json.aspx?AppId=&Query=pete+warden&Sources=Web"

{"SearchResponse":{
  "Version":"2.2",
  "Query":{"SearchTerms":"pete warden"},
  "Web":{
    "Total":276000,"Offset":0,"Results":[
      {"Title":"Pete Warden",
      "Description":"I've had reports of problems running these with the latest
 After Effects CS3. I'm not working with AE at the moment, so I haven't been able to
 investigate and fix the problems.",
      "Url":"http:\/\/petewarden.com\/",
  ...
```

Google Custom Search (*http://code.google.com/apis/customsearch/v1/overview.html*)

As the king of search, Google doesn't have much of an incentive to open up its data to external developers...and it shows. Google killed off the Ajax Search API (*http://code.google.com/edu/ajax/tutorials/ajax-search-api.html#Search*) that allowed access to the same results as the web interface and replaced it with the more restrictive Custom Search (*http://code.google.com/apis/customsearch/v1/overview.html*) version. You'll need to sign up (*http://code.google.com/apis/console/?api=customsearch*) to get access, and you start with a default of only 100 queries per day, with any additional calls requiring approval from the company. You can also only search a specific slice of the Web, which you'll need to specify up front:

```
curl "https://www.googleapis.com/customsearch/v1?\
key=<key>&cx=017576662512468239146:omuauf_lfve&alt=json&\
q=pete%20warden&prettyprint=true"

{"kind": "customsearch#search",
 "url": {
  "type": "application/json",
...
 "items": [
  {
   "kind": "customsearch#result",
   "title": "mana cross pang confidante surplus fine formic beach metallurgy ...",
   "htmlTitle": "mana cross pang confidante surplus fine formic beach metallurgy
\u003cb\u003e...\u003c/b\u003e",
   "link":
"http://www.cs.caltech.edu/courses/cs11/material/advjava/lab4/unsorted_words.txt",
   "displayLink": "www.cs.caltech.edu",
   "snippet": "... phonic phenotype exchangeable Pete pesticide exegete exercise
persuasion  .... lopsided judiciary Lear proverbial warden Sumatra Hempstead
confiscate ...",
  },
...
```

Wikipedia (*http://en.wikipedia.org/wiki/Wikipedia:Database_download*)

Wikipedia doesn't offer an API, but it does offer bulk data downloads of almost everything on the site. One of my favorite uses for this information is extracting the titles of all the articles to create a list of the names of people, places, and concepts to match text against. The hardest part about this is the pollution of the data set with many obscure or foreign titles, so I usually use the traffic statistics that are available as a separate bulk download (*http://dammit.lt/wikistats/*) to restrict my matching to only the most popular topics. Once you've got this shortlist, you can use it to extract interesting words or phrases from free text, without needing to do any more complex semantic analysis.

Google Suggest (*http://answers.oreilly.com/topic/1526-how-to-use-the -google-suggest-api-to-come-up-with-topics-for-answers/*)

Though it's not an official API, the autocomplete feature that's used in Google's tool-bars is a fascinating source of user-generated data. It returns the top ten search terms that begin with the phrase you pass in, along with rough counts for the popularity of each search. The data is accessed through a simple web URL, and it is returned as XML. Unfortunately, since it's not a documented interface, you're probably technically violating Google's terms of service by using it outside of a toolbar, and it would be unwise to call the API too frequently:

```
curl "http://google.com/complete/search?output=toolbar&q=%22San+Francisco+is+"

<?xml version="1.0"?><toplevel>
 <CompleteSuggestion><suggestion data="san francisco is in what county"/>
 <num_queries int="77100000"/></CompleteSuggestion>
 <CompleteSuggestion><suggestion data="san francisco is full of characters"/>
 <num_queries int="20700000"/></CompleteSuggestion>
 <CompleteSuggestion><suggestion data="san francisco is known for"/>
 <num_queries int="122000000"/></CompleteSuggestion>
 <CompleteSuggestion><suggestion data="san francisco is weird"/>
 <num_queries int="6830000"/></CompleteSuggestion>
 <CompleteSuggestion><suggestion data="san francisco is for carnivores"/>
 <num_queries int="103000"/></CompleteSuggestion>
 <CompleteSuggestion><suggestion data="san francisco is boring"/>
 <num_queries int="3330000"/></CompleteSuggestion>
 <CompleteSuggestion>
 <suggestion data="san francisco is the best city in the world"/>
 <num_queries int="63800000"/></CompleteSuggestion>
 <CompleteSuggestion><suggestion data="san francisco is gay"/>
 <num_queries int="24100000"/></CompleteSuggestion>
 <CompleteSuggestion><suggestion data="san francisco is burning"/>
 <num_queries int="11200000"/></CompleteSuggestion>
 <CompleteSuggestion><suggestion data="san francisco is overrated"/>
 <num_queries int="409000"/></CompleteSuggestion>
</toplevel>
```

Wolfram Alpha (*http://products.wolframalpha.com/api/*)

The Wolfram Alpha platform pulls together a very broad range of facts and figures on everything from chemistry (*http://www.wolframalpha.com/examples/Chemistry.html*) to finance (*http://www.wolframalpha.com/examples/MoneyAndFinance.html*). The REST API takes in some search terms as input, and returns an XML document containing the results. The output is a series of sections called *pods*, each containing text and images ready to display to users. Unfortunately there's no easy way to get a machine-readable version of this information, so you can't do further processing on the data within your application. It's still a rich source of supplemental data to add into your own search results, though, which is how Bing is using the service.

If you're a noncommercial user, you can make up to 2,000 queries a month for free, and you can experiment with the interactive API console (*http://products.wolframalpha .com/api/explorer.html*) if you want to explore the service. The commercial rates range between two and six cents a call, depending on the volume. The terms of use (*http:// products.wolframalpha.com/api/termsofuse.html*) prohibit any caching of the data returned from the service and you'll need to sign up (*http://developer.wolframalpha.com/ portal/apisignup.html*) for a key to access it:

```
curl "http://api.wolframalpha.com/v2/query?\
appid=<key>input=General%20Electric&format=image,plaintext,cell,minput"

<?xml version='1.0' encoding='UTF-8'?>
<queryresult success='true'
    error='false'
...
 <pod title='Latest trade'
    scanner='FinancialData'
    id='Quote'
    position='200'
    error='false'
    numsubpods='1'>
  <subpod title=''>
   <plaintext>$19.72(GE | NYSE | Friday 1:00:18 pm PST | 27 hrs ago)</plaintext>
...
```

Locations

Geographic information is such a wide field that it probably deserves its own guide, but here I'm going to focus on the most useful and accessible data sources I've found. All of these take some kind of geographic location, either a place name, an address, or latitude/longitude coordinates, and return additional information about that area.

SimpleGeo (*http://simplegeo.com/docs/api-endpoints/simplegeo-context*)

This is a compendium of useful geographic data, with a simple REST interface to access it. You can use the Context API (*http://simplegeo.com/docs/api-endpoints/simplegeo-con text*) to get additional information about a location and Places (*http://simplegeo.com/ docs/api-endpoints/simplegeo-places*) to find points of interest nearby. There are no rate limits (*http://simplegeo.com/docs/getting-started/introduction#rate-limiting*), but you do have to get an API key and use OAuth to authenticate (*http://developers.simplegeo .com/blog/2011/01/07/two-legged-oauth/*) your calls:

```
http://api.simplegeo.com/1.0/context/37.778381,-122.389388.json

{
    "query":{
       "latitude":37.778381,
       "longitude":-122.389388
    },
```

```
    "timestamp":1291766899.794,
    "weather": {
       "temperature": "65F",
       "conditions": "light haze"
    }, {
    "demographics": {
       "metro_score": 9
    },
    "features":[
        {
          "handle":"SG_4H2GqJDZrcOZAjKGR8qM4D_37.778406_-122.389506",
          "license":"http://creativecommons.org/licenses/by-sa/2.0/",
          "attribution":"(c) OpenStreetMap (http://openstreetmap.org/) and
contributors CC-BY-SA (http://creativecommons.org/licenses/by-sa/2.0/)",
          "classifiers":[
              {
                "type":"Entertainment",
                "category":"Arena",
                "subcategory":"Stadium"
              }
          ],
          "bounds":[
              -122.39115,
              37.777233,
              -122.387775,
              37.779731
          ],
          "abbr":null,
          "name":"AT&T Park",
          "href":"http://api.simplegeo.com/
1.0/features/SG_4H2GqJDZrcOZAjKGR8qM4D_37.778406_-122.389506.json"
      },
    ...
```

Yahoo! (*http://developer.yahoo.com/geo/placemaker/*)

Yahoo! has been a surprising leader in online geo APIs, with Placefinder (*http://devel
oper.yahoo.com/geo/placefinder/*) for converting addresses or place names into coordinates, GeoPlanet (*http://developer.yahoo.com/geo/geoplanet/*) for getting category and
neighborhood information about places, and Placemaker (*http://developer.yahoo.com/
geo/placemaker/*) for analyzing text documents and extracting words or phrases that
represent locations. You'll need to sign up for an app ID (*https://developer.apps.yahoo
.com/wsregapp/*), but after that it's a simple REST/JSON interface.

You can also download a complete list (*http://developer.yahoo.com/geo/geoplanet/
data/*) of the locations that Yahoo has in its database, holding their names and the
WOEID identifier for each. This can be a useful resource for doing offline processing,
though it is a bit hobbled by the lack of any coordinates for the locations:

```
curl "http://where.yahooapis.com/geocode?\
q=1600+Pennsylvania+Avenue,+Washington,+DC&appid=<App ID>&flags=J"

{"ResultSet":{"version":"1.0","Error":0,"ErrorMessage":"No error","Locale":"us_US",
```

```
"Quality":87,"Found":1,"Results":[{
  "quality":85,
  "latitude":"38.898717","longitude":"-77.035974",
  "offsetlat":"38.898590","offsetlon":"-77.035971",
  "radius":500,"name":"","line1":"1600 Pennsylvania Ave NW",
  "line2":"Washington, DC  20006","line3":"",
  "line4":"United States","house":"1600",
  "street":"Pennsylvania Ave NW",
...
```

Google Geocoding API (*http://code.google.com/apis/maps/documentation/ geocoding/*)

You can only use this geocoding API if you're going to display the results on a Google Map (*http://code.google.com/apis/maps/terms.html#section_10_12*), which severely limits its usefulness. There's also a default limit of 2,500 requests per day, though commercial customers get up to 100,000. It doesn't require any key or authentication, and it also supports "reverse geocoding," where you supply a latitude and longitude and get back nearby addresses:

```
curl "http://maps.googleapis.com/maps/api/geocode/json?\
address=1600+Amphitheatre+Parkway,+Mountain+View,+CA&sensor=false"

{ "status": "OK",
  "results": [ {
    "types": [ "street_address" ],
    "formatted_address": "1600 Amphitheatre Pkwy, Mountain View, CA 94043, USA",
    "address_components": [ {
      "long_name": "1600",
      "short_name": "1600",
      "types": [ "street_number" ]
    }, {
      "long_name": "Amphitheatre Pkwy",
      "short_name": "Amphitheatre Pkwy",
      "types": [ "route" ]
    }, {
...
```

CityGrid (*http://docs.citygridmedia.com/display/citygridv1/Search*)

With listings for eighteen million US businesses, this local search engine offers an API to find companies that are near a particular location. You can pass in a general type of business or a particular name and either latitude/longitude coordinates or a place name. The service offers a REST/JSON interface that requires a sign up (*http://developer.city gridmedia.com/member/register*), and the terms of service (*http://developer.citygridme dia.com/apps/tos*) and usage requirements (*http://docs.citygridmedia.com/display/city gridv2/Usage+Requirements*) restrict the service to user-facing applications. CityGrid does offer an unusual ad-driven revenue sharing option (*http://docs.citygridmedia.com/ display/citygridv2/Places+that+Pay*), though, if you meet the criteria:

```
curl "http://api.citygridmedia.com/content/places/v2/search/where?\
where=94117&what=bakery&format=json&publisher=<publisher>&api_key=<key>"

{"results":{"query_id":null,
...
"locations":[{"id":904051,"featured":false,"name":"Blue Front Cafe",
  "address":{"street":"1430 Haight St",
 "city":"San Francisco","state":"CA","postal_code":"94117"},
...
```

Geocoder.us (*http://search.cpan.org/~sderle/Geo-Coder-US/*)

The Geocoder.us (*http://geocoder.us/*) website offers a commercial API for converting US addresses into location coordinates. It costs $50 for 20,000 lookups, but thankfully, Geocoder has also open-sourced the code as a Perl CPAN module (*http://search.cpan .org/~sderle/Geo-Coder-US/*). It's straightforward to install, but the tricky part is populating it with data, since it relies on Tiger/Line data from the US Census. You'll need to hunt around on the Census website (*http://www2.census.gov/geo/tiger/TI GER2007FE/*) to locate the files you need, and then they're a multigigabyte download.

Geodict (*http://github.com/petewarden/geodict/*)

An open source library similar to Yahoo!'s Placemaker API, my project takes in a text string and extracts country, city, and state names from it, along with their coordinates. It's designed to run locally, and it only spots words that are highly likely to represent place names. For example, Yahoo! will flag the "New York" in "New York Times" as a location, whereas Geodict requires a state name to follow it or a location word like *in* or *at* to precede it:

```
./geodict.py -f json < testinput.txt

[{"found_tokens": [{
  "code": "ES", "matched_string": "Spain",
  "lon": -4.0, "end_index": 4, "lat": 40.0,
  "type": "COUNTRY", "start_index": 0}]},
...
```

GeoNames (*http://www.geonames.org/export/ws-overview.html*)

GeoNames has a large number of APIs available for all sorts of geographic queries, based on its database of eight million place names. You can use a simple REST interface with no authentication required, or you can download the entire database under a Creative Commons license if you want to run your own analysis and processing on it. There's some unusual data available, including weather (*http://www.geonames.org/export/JSON-webservices.html#weatherJSON*), ocean names (*http://www.geonames.org/export/web-services.html#ocean*), and elevation (*http://www.geonames.org/export/web-services.html#astergdem*):

```
curl "http://ws.geonames.org/findNearestAddressJSON?lat=37.451&lng=-122.18"
```

```
{"address":{"postalcode":"94025","adminCode2":"081","adminCode1":"CA",
  "street":"Roble Ave","countryCode":"US","lng":"-122.18032",
  "placename":"Menlo Park","adminName2":"San Mateo",
  "distance":"0.04","streetNumber":"671",
  "mtfcc":"S1400","lat":"37.45127","adminName1":"California"}}
```

US Census (*http://www.census.gov/main/www/access.html*)

If you're interested in American locations, the Census site is a mother lode of freely downloadable information. The only problem is that it can be very hard to find what you're looking for on the site. A good place to start for large data sets is the Summary File 100-Percent Data (*http://factfinder.census.gov/servlet/DCGeoSelectServlet?ds_name=DEC_2000_SF1_U*) download interface.

You can select something like ZIP codes or counties in the National Level section (Figure 4).

Figure 4. US Census site

Next, select the statistics that you're interested in (Figure 5).

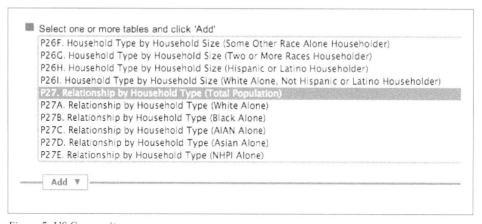

Figure 5. US Census site

Then you'll be able to download that data as a text file. The format is a bit odd, a table with columns separated by "|" (pipe) characters, but with a bit of find-and-replace magic, you can convert them into standard CSV files readable by any spreadsheet.

To ensure privacy, the Census does rearrange its very detailed data in some cases, without invalidating its statistical significance. For example, if there's only one Iranian doctor in Boulder, Colorado, that person may be included in a neighboring city's data instead and swapped with an equivalent person's information, so the overall statistics on income, etc. are unaffected.

There's also a wealth of shape data available (*http://www.census.gov/geo/www/cob/bdy _files.html*), giving detailed coordinates for the boundaries of US counties, states, cities, and congressional districts.

Zillow Neighborhoods (*http://www.zillow.com/howto/api/neighborhood -boundaries.htm*)

The only US boundary that the Census doesn't offer is neighborhoods. Thankfully, the Zillow real estate site has made its neighborhood data available as Creative Commons–licensed downloads (Figure 6).

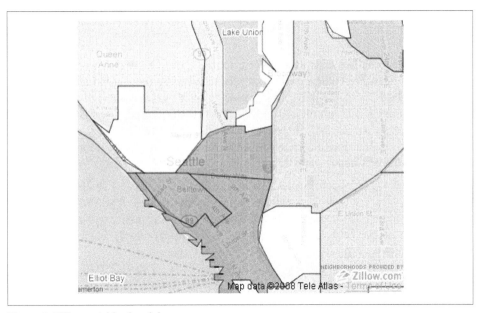

Figure 6. Zillow neighborhood data

Natural Earth (*http://www.naturalearthdata.com/*)

Natural Earth offers a very clean, accurate, and detailed public domain collection of country and province boundaries for the entire planet, available for download in bulk (Figure 7). You'll need some geo knowledge to convert them into a usable form, but it's not too much of a challenge. For example, you could load the shapefiles into Post-GIS (*http://postgis.refractions.net/*) and then easily run reverse geo-code queries to discover which country and state a point lies within.

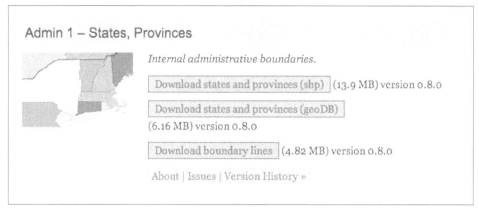

Figure 7. Natural Earth data

US National Weather Service (*http://www.weather.gov/forecasts/xml/rest .php*)

There are other weather APIs available through Yahoo! (*http://developer.yahoo.com/ weather/*) and Weather Underground (*http://wiki.wunderground.com/index.php/API_- _XML*), but the NWS is the only organization to offer one without significant restrictions on commercial and mobile usage. It only covers the United States, unfortunately. The NWS offers a REST/XML interface, and it doesn't require any authentication or registration, though it does ask that you cache results for any point for an hour, since that's the update frequency of its data.

You can access either current conditions or forecasts for up to a week ahead, and you can search by city, zip code, or latitude/longitude coordinates. If you're interested in bulk sets of longer-term historical data on weather, the University of Nebraska has a great guide available (*http://www.drought.unl.edu/dm/source.html*). Some of the information stretches back thousands of years, thanks to tree rings:

```
curl "http://www.weather.gov/forecasts/xml/sample_products/browser_interface/\
ndfdXMLclient.php?lat=38.99&lon=-77.01&product=time-series&\
begin=2004-01-01T00:00:00&end=2013-04-20T00:00:00&maxt=maxt&mint=mint"

<?xml version="1.0"?>
<dwml version="1.0" xmlns:xsd="http://www.w3.org/2001/XMLSchema"
 xmlns:xsi="http://www.w3.org/2001/XMLSchema-instance"
 xsi:noNamespaceSchemaLocation=
 "http://www.nws.noaa.gov/forecasts/xml/DWMLgen/schema/DWML.xsd">
  <head>
...
  </head>
  <data>
    <location>
      <location-key>point1</location-key>
      <point latitude="38.99" longitude="-77.01"/>
```

```
      </location>
  ...
      <parameters applicable-location="point1">
        <temperature type="maximum" units="Fahrenheit" time-layout="k-p24h-n8-1">
          <name>Daily Maximum Temperature</name>
          <value>38</value>
          <value>33</value>
          <value>41</value>
          <value>41</value>
          <value>35</value>
          <value>32</value>
          <value>30</value>
          <value>35</value>
        </temperature>
        <temperature type="minimum" units="Fahrenheit" time-layout="k-p24h-n7-2">
          <name>Daily Minimum Temperature</name>
          <value>22</value>
          <value>28</value>
          <value>34</value>
          <value>22</value>
          <value>24</value>
          <value>17</value>
          <value>20</value>
        </temperature>
      </parameters>
    </data>
  </dwml>
```

OpenStreetMap (*http://wiki.openstreetmap.org/wiki/Planet.osm*)

The volunteers at OpenStreetMap have created a somewhat-chaotic but comprehensive set of geographic information, and you can download everything they've gathered as a single massive file. One unique strength is the coverage of areas in the developing world that are absent from commercial databases, and since it's so easy to change, even US locations are often more up-to-date with recent changes than more traditional maps. The downside of the system is that it's designed for navigation, not analysis, so a lot of information about administrative boundaries and other nonphysical attributes is missing. The Nominatim project (*http://wiki.openstreetmap.org/wiki/Nominatim/Installation*) attempts to organize the data into a form you can use to look up street addresses, but the lack of good coverage of things like postal codes limits its usefulness. Reconstructing some structure from the soup of roads and points is also computationally very taxing, easily taking a couple weeks of computation time on a high-end machine.

If you're only working in a more limited geographic region, you may want to look at the Cloudmade extracts (*http://downloads.cloudmade.com/*), which contain subsets for different areas and attributes.

MaxMind (*http://www.maxmind.com/app/worldcities*)

This is one of the simplest but most useful data sets for geographic applications. It's a CSV file containing information on 2.7 million cities and towns around the world. It has the latitude and longitude coordinates, region, country, and alternate names for all of them, and the population for many thanks to Stefan Helder's data (*http://www.world -gazetteer.com/*). You can just load this file into your favorite database, index by the key you want to query on, and you've got a perfectly workable local service for working with addresses and other locations:

```
...
us,new woodstock,New Woodstock,NY,,42.8483333,-75.8547222
us,new york,New York,NY,8107916,40.7141667,-74.0063889
us,new york mills,New York Mills,NY,,43.1052778,-75.2916667
us,newark,Newark,NY,9365,43.0466667,-77.0955556
...
```

Companies

CrunchBase (*http://groups.google.com/group/crunchbase-api/web/api-v1 -documentation*)

TechCrunch has accumulated information on more than 50,000 companies and 70,000 people and has made it available both through a web interface and a simple REST/ JSON API. You don't need to authenticate, and it's all under a Creative Commons license. There aren't any official bulk downloads available, but I created the Crunch-Crawl (*http://github.com/petewarden/crunchcrawl*) project to use the API to pull down information about all companies in the system.

To get information about a particular company, you'll first need to search on its name to find the CrunchBase ID; then you can access the full set of data. As you might imagine, the database has excellent coverage of technology companies but very little on other industries:

```
curl "http://api.crunchbase.com/v/1/company/facebook.js"

{"name": "Facebook",
 "permalink": "facebook",
 "crunchbase_url": "http://www.crunchbase.com/company/facebook",
 "homepage_url": "http://facebook.com",
 "blog_url": "http://blog.facebook.com",
 "blog_feed_url": "http://blog.facebook.com/atom.php",
 "twitter_username": "facebook",
...
```

ZoomInfo (*http://developer.zoominfo.com/*)

Covering around four million US companies, ZoomInfo has broader coverage and is less tech-centric than CrunchBase. It offers a REST interface with XML output, with only 2,000 queries a day permitted, and terms of service (*http://developer.zoominfo.com/API_terms_of_use*) that require branding on any services you create using it:

```
curl "http://api.zoominfo.com/PartnerAPI/XmlOutput.aspx?\
query_type=company_search_query&pc=<key>&companyName=Facebook"

<?xml version="1.0" encoding="utf-8"?>
...
<TotalResults>84</TotalResults><CompanySearchResults>
<CompanyRecord><CompanyID>32394811</CompanyID>
<ZoomCompanyUrl>http://www.zoominfo.com/Search/CompanyDetail.aspx?
CompanyID=32394811&amp;cs=QEB7k47oc&amp;pc=publicapi
</ZoomCompanyUrl>
<CompanyName>Facebook</CompanyName>
<CompanyTicker/>
<Website>www.facebook.com</Website>
<CompanyAddress><City>Palo Alto</City><State>CA</State><CountryCode>USA</CountryCode>
```

Hoover's (*http://developer.hoovers.com/docs34/companyrest*)

With the most comprehensive database of company information, the Hoover's API is heavily geared toward enterprise-level users. Hoover's does offer a REST/JSON interface, somewhat strangely using HTTP Basic Authentication headers for the key information. You only get three months of free access to the API (for testing purposes) before you have to talk to the sales staff about your application, but at least you can sign up initially online with no wait. To get information about a company, do a search to retrieve the company ID within the service. Then you can pull down address, revenue, and employee count, along with lots of other statistics.

Yahoo! Finance (*http://www.gummy-stuff.org/Yahoo-data.htm*)

For many years, Yahoo! has let you look up trading information for companies based on their stock tickers. This isn't an official API, so it may be removed or altered at any point, and the terms under which you can use the information are unclear. I'm including it despite those warnings, because it does make some unique information available. Unusually, it returns its results as a CSV file, which is great if you want to run it through further spreadsheet processing, but which will require a little parsing work from a scripting language:

```
curl "http://download.finance.yahoo.com/d/quotes.csv?\
s=BBDB.TO+NT.TO+GE+MSFT&f=snl1d1t1ohgdr"

"BBD-B.TO","BOMBARDIER INC., ",5.26,"1/7/2011","4:40pm",5.40,5.41,5.24,0.10,15.91
"NT.TO","NT.TO",0.00,"N/A","11:-40am",N/A,N/A,N/A,N/A,N/A
```

```
"GE","General Electric ",18.43,"1/7/2011","4:00pm",18.58,18.66,18.20,0.46,20.26
"MSFT","Microsoft Corpora",28.60,"1/7/2011","4:00pm",28.64,28.74,28.25,0.55,12.42
```

IP Addresses

You almost always know the IP address of the machine a user is connecting to your web service from, and it's possible to guess a lot of information based on that number. In fact, it's so powerful that it's treated as personally identifiable information in the EU, so for privacy-sensitive applications I'd recommend you remove IP addresses from your logs entirely (*http://bluwiki.com/go/How_to_remove_IP_addresses#Micro-howto _:_how_to_get_rid_of_IP_addresses_in_Apache.27s_logs*).

You do need to be careful, though, since the information derived from IP addresses is unreliable. In particular it's not a good idea to make hard-and-fast decisions based on the geographic results. It can be very useful to use that information to intelligently set defaults for languages or home locations, though, as long as the user can correct them subsequently.

MaxMind (*http://www.maxmind.com/app/geolitecity*)

The GeoLite City database by MaxMind is one of my all-time favorite resources. It's a comprehensive data set listing the city and country locations of a large number of IP addresses, released under a data license (*http://geolite.maxmind.com/download/geoip/ database/LICENSE.txt*) that does require credit but is otherwise very open. It also comes bundled with a set of APIs for a lot of different languages that make it easy to do the IP to location lookup from within your own programs. GeoLite City also offers a richer commercial data set that you can drop into a system using the free files, without requiring any code changes.

Infochimps (*http://api.infochimps.com/describe/web/an/de/ demographics*)

Taking the geolocation idea a step further, Infochimps offers up demographic information on the area that a visitor is living in. It appears to rely on US Census data, since it returns only language information for other countries. You could use this to better target offers or otherwise customize the user experience on your site, though obviously the information will be pretty approximate:

```
curl "http://api.infochimps.com/web/an/de/demographics.json?\
apikey=api_test-W1cipwpcdu9Cbd9pmm8D4Cjc469&ip=67.195.115.39"
```

```
{ "men":2568,"women":2640,"w35_49":787,"m35_49":806,"kids":890,
  "w18_34":700,"teens":515,"m18_34":752,
  "rank":6,"lang":"english","second_langs":"?","households":2476}
```

Books, Films, Music, and Products

Amazon (*https://affiliate-program.amazon.com/gp/advertising/api/detail/main.html*)

Amazon has one of the largest catalogs of products in the world, and as long as you're directing users to its site (*https://affiliate-program.amazon.com/gp/advertising/api/detail/agreement.html*), it allows you to access its information through an API. It's somewhat fiddly to use, since it was originally all SOAP-based and relies on XML and computing URL signatures, but there are a lot of libraries that can help (*http://aws.amazon.com/code/Product%20Advertising%20API?_encoding=UTF8&jiveRedirect=1*). If you're trying to get information on real-world products, the Barcode/UPC search capability (*http://stackoverflow.com/questions/1221407/do-the-amazon-web-service-apis-support-barcode-upc-queries*) might be particularly useful. Be careful, as there are a few restrictions hidden in the terms of service, particularly around mobile applications.

If you find the API too inflexible, you could follow in the footsteps of the shopping search engines and write a web crawler that gathers the information from Amazon's HTML pages. Check their *robots.txt* to ensure that it's still permissible, but currently it's open to this sort of use, though I don't know of any open source examples showing how to do it.

Google Shopping (*http://code.google.com/apis/shopping/search/v1/getting_started.html*)

Like Amazon's, this API has been designed to support websites that want to display products to their visitors in the hope of benefiting from affiliate fees. As such, its terms of service prohibit "scraping, database building, or the creation of permanent copies" of the information you retrieve. It offers a variety of ways to track down products, including by UPC or ISBN codes:

```
curl "https://www.googleapis.com/shopping/search/v1/public/products?key=<key>&\
country=US&q=digital+camera"

{"kind": "shopping#products",
...
 "items": [
  {
   "kind": "shopping#product",
   "id": "tag:google.com,2010:shopping/products/10048/16324480569195213774",
   "selfLink": "https://www.googleapis.com/shopping/search/v1/
public/products/10048/gid/16324480569195213774",
    "product": {
     "googleId": "16324480569195213774",
     "author": {
      "name": "Staples",
      "accountId": "10048"
```

```
        },
        "creationTime": "2010-04-18T16:18:40.000Z",
        "modificationTime": "2011-01-07T19:15:40.000Z",
        "country": "US",
        "language": "en",
        "title": "Olympus Stylus TOUGH-3000 Digital Camera, Pink",
        "description": "The STYLUS TOUGH-3000 is loads of fun for the whole family
    ...
```

Google Book Search (*http://code.google.com/apis/books/docs/gdata/ developers_guide_protocol.html*)

If you're looking specifically for a book, this second API from Google will probably be more useful than the more general Shopping engine. You can do a search using all the advanced operators (*http://books.google.com/advanced_book_search*) from the Book Search web interface, looking for titles, authors, or ISBNs. You don't have to authenticate or get an API key to use this, and the results are available as a public Atom-format RSS feed, so it's unclear what restrictions there are on its use:

```
curl "http://books.google.com/books/feeds/volumes?q=instrumentality+of+mankind"
```

Netflix (*http://developer.netflix.com/*)

If you're dealing with movies or TV shows, this API offers a lot of information. The formal terms of service (*http://developer.netflix.com/page/Api_terms_of_use*) are reasonable, and the ten commandments version on the main page (*http://developer.netflix .com/*) should be an example to API providers everywhere, making clear what Netflix's goals are without clouding them in legalese—"Delight Customers," "Handle Content with Care," and "Respect the Netflix Brand." The rate limits (*http://developer.netflix .com/docs/Security*) might be a little tight, at 5,000 per day, but that's per user if you're doing calls for logged-in Netflix accounts. Unfortunately, almost all of the methods do require three-legged OAuth authorization, apart from auto-complete. The good news is that you can download the entire 1.3GB, 130,000+ title database through this OAuth-required link: *http://api.netflix.com/catalog/titles/full?v=2.0*.

Having the bulk data available means you can integrate it very flexibly with your own backend. It still comes with the same restrictions as the API, but these seem well-crafted to cramp innovation as little as possible.

Yahoo! Music (*http://developer.yahoo.com/music/*)

This service lets you query both a large back catalog of music and information on the current charts using YQL. You're limited to 5,000 queries a day, and the information you get back on artists isn't very extensive, but it's simple to access, as it doesn't require any authentication:

```
curl "http://query.yahooapis.com/v1/public/yql?\
q=select%20*%20from%20music.artist.search%20where%20keyword%3D'Rihanna'&format=json"
```

```
{"query":{"count":"4","created":"2011-01-09T16:45:20Z","lang":"en-US","results":{
  "Artist":[{"catzillaID":"1927869111","flags":"124547","hotzillaID":"1809845326",
 "id":"19712698","name":"Rihanna","rating":"-1","trackCount":"453",
 "url":"http://new.music.yahoo.com/rihanna/",
 "website":"http://rihannanow.com","ItemInfo":{"Relevancy":{"index":"465"}}}},
 ...
```

Musicbrainz (*http://musicbrainz.org/doc/MusicBrainz_Database #Download*)

This site has assembled a large collection of information on music artists and works, and it has made the results available for download under an open license (*http://musicbrainz.org/doc/MusicBrainz_License*). It's reusable under a mixture of public domain and Creative Commons licensing, depending on the attributes you're looking at.

You can also access the same data through the online REST/XML API, where you can look up artists and works and get back quite a lot of information, not only about the people and albums, but also about their relationships to one another:

```
curl "http://musicbrainz.org/ws/1/artist/?type=xml&name=Tori+Amos"
```

```
<?xml version="1.0" encoding="UTF-8"?>
...
<artist type="Person" id="c0b2500e-0cef-4130-869d-732b23ed9df5" ext:score="100">
<name>Tori Amos</name><sort-name>Amos, Tori</sort-name>
<life-span begin="1963-08-22"/></artist>
...
```

The Movie DB (*http://api.themoviedb.org/2.1*)

A rival site to the well-established IMDB, Movie DB has an API that gives you access to details on a wide range of movies. The terms of service (*http://api.themoviedb.org/2.1/terms-of-use*) aren't too constraining, with no requirement that your project be immediately end-user-facing, though Movie DB does discourage caching of data. I couldn't find any information on rate limits:

```
curl "http://api.themoviedb.org/2.1/Movie.search/en/xml/<key>/Transformers"
```

```
<?xml version="1.0" encoding="UTF-8"?>
<OpenSearchDescription xmlns:opensearch="http://a9.com/-/spec/opensearch/1.1/">
  <opensearch:Query searchTerms="transformers"/>
  <opensearch:totalResults>8</opensearch:totalResults>
  <movies>
    <movie>
      <score></score>
      <popularity>3</popularity>
      <translated></translated>
      <adult>false</adult>
```

```
      <language>en</language>
      <original_name>Transformers</original_name>
      <name>Transformers</name>
      <alternative_name>The Transformers</alternative_name>
      <type>movie</type>
      <id>1858</id>
      <imdb_id>tt0418279</imdb_id>
      <url>http://www.themoviedb.org/movie/1858</url>
      <votes>61</votes>
      <rating>7.4</rating>
      <certification>PG-13</certification>
      <overview>Young teenager Sam Witwicky becomes involved in the ancient struggle
between two extraterrestrial factions...
      <released>2007-07-04</released>
  ...
```

Freebase (*http://wiki.freebase.com/wiki/API*)

Freebase has a large collection of user-contributed information on films, TV shows, and other media. Its coverage is a bit patchy, since it depends on the enthusiasm of volunteers, but no authentication is required to access its REST/JSON interface and it has a flexible query language. You do need to be a little careful crafting your queries, since it appears to restrict you to a single query at a time, so if you accidentally create a long-running one by selecting too many rows, you'll be blocked until it completes.

If you want to run your own offline analysis, you can also grab snapshots of entire database as a multigigabyte file: *http://download.freebase.com/datadumps/latest/*:

```
curl "http://api.freebase.com/api/service/mqlread?\
query=\{%22query%22%3A%5B\{%22id%22%3Anull%2C%22name%22%3A%22The+Wicker+Man\
%22%2C%22type%22%3A%22%2Ffilm%2Ffilm%22\}%5D\}"
```

```
{ "code": "/api/status/ok",
  "result": [
    {
      "id": "/en/the_wicker_man",
      "name": "The Wicker Man",
      "type": "/film/film"
    },
    {
      "id": "/en/the_wicker_man_2006",
      "name": "The Wicker Man",
      "type": "/film/film"
    }
  ],
  "status": "200 OK",
  "transaction_id": "cache;cache04.p01.sjc1:8101;2011-01-09T17:35:11Z;0012"
}
```

The information you need, when and where you need it.

With Safari Books Online, you can:

Access the contents of thousands of technology and business books

- Quickly search over 7000 books and certification guides
- Download whole books or chapters in PDF format, at no extra cost, to print or read on the go
- Copy and paste code
- Save up to 35% on O'Reilly print books
- **New!** Access mobile-friendly books directly from cell phones and mobile devices

Stay up-to-date on emerging topics before the books are published

- Get on-demand access to evolving manuscripts.
- Interact directly with authors of upcoming books

Explore thousands of hours of video on technology and design topics

- Learn from expert video tutorials
- Watch and replay recorded conference sessions

Get even more for your money.

Join the O'Reilly Community, and register the O'Reilly books you own. It's free, and you'll get:

- $4.99 ebook upgrade offer
- 40% upgrade offer on O'Reilly print books
- Membership discounts on books and events
- Free lifetime updates to ebooks and videos
- Multiple ebook formats, DRM FREE
- Participation in the O'Reilly community
- Newsletters
- Account management
- 100% Satisfaction Guarantee

Signing up is easy:

1. **Go to: oreilly.com/go/register**
2. **Create an O'Reilly login.**
3. **Provide your address.**
4. **Register your books.**

Note: English-language books only

To order books online:
oreilly.com/store

For questions about products or an order:
orders@oreilly.com

To sign up to get topic-specific email announcements and/or news about upcoming books, conferences, special offers, and new technologies:
elists@oreilly.com

For technical questions about book content:
booktech@oreilly.com

To submit new book proposals to our editors:
proposals@oreilly.com

O'Reilly books are available in multiple DRM-free ebook formats. For more information:
oreilly.com/ebooks

O'REILLY®

Spreading the knowledge of innovators   oreilly.com

Lightning Source UK Ltd.
Milton Keynes UK
UKHW031845010323
417874UK00007B/240